# CHILE 2016 HUMAN RIGHTS REPORT

## EXECUTIVE SUMMARY

Chile is a constitutional multiparty democracy. In 2013 citizens elected Michelle Bachelet to be president in an election that observers considered free and fair. The country also held concurrent legislative elections. President Bachelet assumed office in March 2014.

Civilian authorities maintained effective control over the security forces.

The principal human rights problems concerned harsh conditions in some prisons; violence and discrimination against women and children, and against lesbian, gay, bisexual, transgender, and intersex (LGBTI) persons; and societal conflict and discrimination against indigenous populations.

The government took steps to investigate and prosecute officials who committed abuses.

## Section 1. Respect for the Integrity of the Person, Including Freedom from:

### a. Arbitrary Deprivation of Life and other Unlawful or Politically Motivated Killings

There were no reports that the government or its agents committed arbitrary or unlawful killings.

As of November 2015 according to the Ministry of the Interior, a total of 1,373 former military and law enforcement officials had been charged or convicted of complicity in murder or disappearance during the Pinochet government years (1973-90).

On July 20, the Supreme Court upheld on appeal the convictions of former Army officer Pedro Espinoza and former Air Force civilian Rafael Gonzalez for the 1973 killings of U.S. citizens Charles Horman and Frank Teruggi and increased the sentences to 15 years of prison for Espinoza and three years of probation for Gonzalez. The court also upheld awards of financial compensation of 130 million pesos ($190,000) for Joyce Horman and 100 million pesos ($146,000) for Janis Teruggi, the next of kin of the deceased.

## b. Disappearance

There were no reports of politically motivated disappearances.

On March 4, Appellate Judge Jorge Zepeda dismissed the case against eight former members of the police and the army who were accused of being complicit in the 1985 disappearance of U.S. citizen Boris Weisfeiler. The judge ruled that while the evidence presented indicated that kidnapping and obstruction of justice did take place, the statute of limitations for prosecuting those crimes had run out. In his decision, Zepeda stated that the defense proved that each of the accused acted of personal volition and not under orders. Therefore, it was inappropriate to classify the death as a crime against humanity, which would have suspended the statute of limitations. The State Defense Council, the Human Rights Program of the Ministry of the Interior, and the family of the victim filed an appeal of this decision, which remained pending at year's end.

## c. Torture and Other Cruel, Inhuman, or Degrading Treatment or Punishment

Although the constitution and law prohibit such practices, there were reports of excessive force, abuse, and degrading treatment by law enforcement officers. In its 2015 annual *Human Rights Report*, the University of Diego Portales published statistics showing that during the period of 2006-14, state prosecutors applied the charge of torture 846 times, and nearly 50 percent of those accusations corresponded to acts committed by correctional officers working within the prison system. A November 11 law updated the criminal code to specify further the elements of the crimes of torture and cruel, inhuman and degrading treatment. The revised code increased penalties for these crimes in line with international norms.

**Prison and Detention Center Conditions**

Conditions in some prisons were harsh, as several antiquated prisons offered substandard sanitary conditions, medical services, heating and ventilation. Human rights organizations reported that violence, including torture, occurred. Violence among inmates also was common.

Physical Conditions: Some prison facilities were antiquated and offered substandard sanitary conditions, inadequate food, and insufficient medical services. Inadequate heating in some prisons remained a serious problem, and inadequate lighting and ventilation also affected inmates at some prisons. The government reported that access to potable water was limited in several prisons.  Violence in prisons was common.  The nongovernmental organization (NGO) Paz Ciudadana reported that prison inmates were 29 times more likely than the general population to be a victim of homicide.

On September 26, a fight among inmates in the South Santiago Center for Preventive Detention left two inmates dead and more than 100 injured, including six inmates taken to an outside hospital for treatment.

Administration:  Independent government authorities, including the National Institute of Human Rights (INDH), a government body, generally investigated credible allegations and documented the results in a publicly accessible manner.  The government usually investigated and monitored prison and detention center conditions.  Some NGOs, including the Center for Studies on Public Safety at the Institute for Public Affairs at the University of Chile, expressed concern over the potential for conflict of interest:  They noted that the Human Rights Unit of the Gendarmeria (the corrections officers corps), served as the investigating body of first instance for complaints of violations by corrections officers but appeared to lack the administrative and political support within the institution necessary to fully execute its duties.

Independent Monitoring:  The government permitted prison visits by independent human rights observers, and such visits took place at both government and privately operated facilities.  Prisoner and human rights groups continued to investigate alleged use of abuse or excessive force against detainees, and media covered some of the allegations.

Improvements:  The government made a concerted, long-term effort to relieve prison overcrowding; many prisons that were grossly overcrowded in 2010 were now at capacity.

**d. Arbitrary Arrest or Detention**

The constitution prohibits arbitrary arrest and detention, and the government generally observed these prohibitions.

**Role of the Police and Security Apparatus**

The Carabineros and the investigative police (PDI) have legal responsibility for law enforcement and maintenance of order, including migration and border enforcement, within the country. The Ministry of the Interior oversees both forces. The INDH monitors complaints and allegations of abuse.

Civilian authorities generally maintained effective control over the Carabineros and the PDI, and the government has mechanisms to investigate and punish abuse and corruption. The military justice system investigates alleged abuses by Carabineros, and the civilian criminal justice system investigates allegations of abuse by PDI officers. A November 11 law defining torture in the criminal code requires all alleged cases of torture or cruel, inhuman, and degrading treatment by any state actor be investigated by the civilian criminal justice system. The NGO Human Rights Watch reported concern that military courts were not fully transparent or independent.

**Arrest Procedures and Treatment of Detainees**

Only public officials expressly authorized by law may arrest or detain citizens and generally did so openly with warrants based on sufficient evidence brought before an independent judiciary. Authorities must immediately inform a prosecutor of an arrest and generally did so.

The prosecutor must open an investigation, receive a statement from the detainee, and ensure that the detainee is held at a local police station until the detention control hearing. Detention control hearings are held twice daily, allowing for a judicial determination of the legality of the detention within 24 hours of arrest. Detainees must be informed of their rights, including the right to an attorney and the right to remain silent until an attorney is present. Public defenders are provided for detainees who do not hire their own lawyer. Authorities must expedite notification of the detention to family members. If authorities do not inform detainees of their rights upon detention, the judge can declare the process unlawful during the detention control hearing.

The law allows judges to set bail, grant provisional liberty, or order continued detention as necessary for the investigation or the protection of the prisoner or the public.

The law affords detainees 30 minutes of immediate and subsequent daily access to a lawyer (in the presence of a prison guard) and to a doctor to verify their physical condition. Regular visits by family members are allowed.

<u>Detainee's Ability to Challenge Lawfulness of Detention before a Court</u>:  Persons arrested or detained are entitled to challenge the legal basis or arbitrary nature of their detention and obtain prompt release and may sue for compensation if found to have been unlawfully detained by judicial error.

## e. Denial of Fair Public Trial

The constitution provides for an independent judiciary, and the government generally respected judicial independence.

## Trial Procedures

The constitution and law provide for the right to a fair public trial, and an independent judiciary generally enforced this right.

Defendants enjoy a presumption of innocence and have a right of appeal.  They have the right to be informed promptly of charges, to have time to prepare their defense, and not to be compelled to testify.  National and regional prosecutors investigate crimes, formulate charges, and prosecute cases.  Three-judge panels form the court of first instance.  The process is oral and adversarial; trials are public; defendants have the right to be present and consult with an attorney in a timely manner; and judges rule on guilt and dictate sentences.  Defendants have the right to free interpretation as necessary from the moment charged through all appeals.  Court records, rulings, and findings were generally accessible to the public.

The law provides for the right to legal counsel, and public defenders' offices across the country provided professional legal counsel to anyone seeking such assistance. When human rights organizations or family members requested, the NGO Corporation for the Promotion and Defense of the Rights of the People and other lawyers working pro bono assisted detainees during interrogation and trial. Defendants may confront or question adverse witnesses and present witnesses and evidence on their behalf, although the law provides for secret witnesses in certain circumstances.  Defendants and their attorneys generally have access to government-held evidence relevant to their cases.  The law extends these rights to all defendants.

For crimes committed prior to the implementation of the 2005 judicial reforms, criminal proceedings are inquisitorial rather than adversarial.  As of December 1, inquisitorial criminal court remained open and had an extensive wait for trials.

**Political Prisoners and Detainees**

There were no reports of political prisoners or detainees, although some indigenous Mapuche convicted of criminal offenses claimed to be political prisoners.

**Civil Judicial Procedures and Remedies**

There is an independent and impartial judiciary in civil matters, which permits individuals to seek civil remedies for human rights violations; however, the civil justice system retained antiquated and inefficient procedures.  The average civil trial lasted approximately five years, and civil suits could continue for decades.  Administrative and judicial remedies are available for alleged wrongs.  Cases involving violations of an individual's human rights may be submitted through petitions by individuals or organizations to the Inter-American Commission of Human Rights (IACHR), which in turn may submit the case to the Inter-American Court of Human Rights.  The court may order civil remedies including fair compensation to the individual injured.

**f. Arbitrary or Unlawful Interference with Privacy, Family, Home, or Correspondence**

The constitution prohibits such actions, and there were no reports that the government failed to respect these prohibitions.

**Section 2. Respect for Civil Liberties, Including:**

**a. Freedom of Speech and Press**

The constitution provides for freedom of speech and press, and the government generally respected these rights.  An independent press, an effective judiciary, and a functioning democratic political system combined to promote freedom of speech and press.

**Internet Freedom**

The government did not restrict or disrupt access to the internet or censor online content, and there were no credible reports that the government monitored private online communications without appropriate legal authority.  According to Internet

World Statistics, approximately 80 percent of the population had access to the internet.

**Academic Freedom and Cultural Events**

There were no government restrictions on academic freedom or cultural events.

**b. Freedom of Peaceful Assembly and Association**

The law provides for the freedoms of assembly and association, and the government generally respected these rights.

**c. Freedom of Religion**

See the Department of State's *International Religious Freedom Report* at www.state.gov/religiousfreedomreport/.

**d. Freedom of Movement, Internally Displaced Persons, Protection of Refugees, and Stateless Persons**

The constitution provides for freedom of internal movement, foreign travel, emigration, and repatriation, and the government generally respected these rights.

The government cooperated with the Office of the UN High Commissioner for Refugees and other humanitarian organizations in providing protection and assistance to internally displaced persons, refugees, returning refugees, asylum seekers, stateless persons, or other persons of concern.

**Protection of Refugees**

Access to Asylum:  The law provides for the granting of asylum or refugee status, and the government has established a system for providing protection to refugees, including access to education and health care.  The country had fewer than 2,000 refugees recognized by the government.

**Section 3. Freedom to Participate in the Political Process**

The law provides citizens the ability to choose their government through free and fair periodic elections held by secret ballot and based on universal and equal suffrage.

**Elections and Political Participation**

<u>Recent Elections</u>:  In December 2013 voters elected Michele Bachelet president in a free and fair election.  In November 2013 voters elected 20 of 38 senators and all members of the Chamber of Deputies in elections considered free and fair.  Members of regional councils also were elected nationwide for the first time in 2013.

<u>Participation of Women and Minorities</u>:  In 2015, as part of a larger reform to the electoral processes, the legislature passed a law to provide for greater gender parity among elected officials by requiring that political parties present at least 40 percent female candidates for national public office.  Although the gender quota did not apply in the 2016 municipal elections, there was a 4 percent increase in women candidates for mayor presented over the previous 2012 municipal election cycle.  Only 12 percent of mayors elected in 2016 were women, the lowest percentage since 2000.

Self-identified indigenous people were elected to public office at the municipal level but not at the national level, in part due to cultural and institutional barriers (see section 6, Indigenous People).

**Section 4. Corruption and Lack of Transparency in Government**

The law provides criminal penalties for corruption by officials, and the government generally implemented these laws effectively, although officials sometimes engaged in corrupt practices with impunity.  There were isolated reports of government corruption during the year.

<u>Corruption</u>:  On June 16, authorities placed Senator Jaime Orpis in pretrial detention on charges of bribery, tax fraud, and money laundering in connection with his vote on a controversial fishing quota law.  Orpis remained under house arrest and the case remained pending at year's end.  Separately, the large financial services organization, Penta Group, and the lithium producer Soquimich, remained under investigation at year's end for alleged illegal political campaign donations.  Prosecutors assert that the organizations evaded taxes by claiming campaign donations as business expenses.

Based on the 2015 recommendations by a government-appointed anticorruption commission, the government passed several laws to improve transparency during the year, including a campaign finance law that establishes limits to private financial contributions to political campaigns and increases the enforcement capacity of the election oversight board.  Additionally, the government passed a law increasing penalties for collusion, including jail time and higher fines, which was widely perceived to be the government's response to allegations that pharmacies, the poultry industry, and toilet paper manufacturers engaged in price fixing.

Financial Disclosure:  Law and regulation require income and asset disclosure by appointed and elected officials.  Declarations are made available to the public and there are administrative sanctions for noncompliance.  On January 5, the president signed into law a provision that expanded the number of public trust positions required to release financial disclosure, mandated disclosure in greater detail, and allowed for stronger penalties for noncompliance.

Public Access to Information:  The constitution provides for public access to government information, and the law was effectively implemented.  The requirement to provide public access to information applies to ministries; regional, provincial, and municipal level governments; the armed forces, police, and public security forces; and public enterprises where the state owns more than 50 percent or holds a majority of appointments on the board of directors.  The law lists five exceptions to disclosure.  Responses to requests for information must be delivered within 20 business days, and there is no cost for making a request.  In cases of noncompliance, the head of the organization is subject to a fine amounting to approximately 20 to 50 percent of his or her monthly salary.  The autonomous Transparency Council serves as an arbitrator in cases in which requests for information are denied, and it makes binding rulings as to whether or not a determination not to release information was correct.

**Section 5. Governmental Attitude Regarding International and Nongovernmental Investigation of Alleged Violations of Human Rights**

A number of domestic and international human rights groups generally operated without government restriction, investigating and publishing their findings on human rights cases.  Government officials were generally cooperative and responsive to their views.

Government Human Rights Bodies:  The INDH operated independently, issued public statements, and proposed changes to government agencies or policies to promote and protect human rights.  In its 2015 report, the INDH took an in-depth look at the human rights impact of environmental degradation, corruption, and poverty, among other themes.

The Senate and Chamber of Deputies have standing human rights committees responsible for drafting human rights legislation.

## Section 6. Discrimination, Societal Abuses, and Trafficking in Persons

### Women

<u>Rape and Domestic Violence</u>:  The law criminalizes rape, including spousal rape. Penalties for rape range from five to 15 years' imprisonment, and the government generally enforced the law when violations were reported.  There was no indication of police or judicial reluctance to act.  The law criminalizes both physical and psychological domestic violence and protects the privacy and safety of the victim making the charge of rape or domestic violence.  Nonetheless, experts believed that many rape and domestic violence cases went unreported due to fear of further violence, retribution, and social stigma.  According to the Ministry of Women and Gender Equality, one in three women had suffered some kind of domestic violence.

Family courts handle cases of domestic violence and penalize offenders with fines up to 556,680 pesos ($821).  Additional sanctions include eviction of the offender from the residence shared with the survivor, restraining orders, confiscation of firearms, and court-ordered counseling.  Cases of habitual psychological abuse and physical abuse cases in which there are physical injuries are prosecuted in the criminal justice system.  Penalties are based on the gravity of injuries and range from 61 to 540 days' imprisonment.

The government continued to campaign against domestic violence, focusing its outreach efforts particularly through social media, and launching a video campaign called "Chile sin Femicidios" (Chile without Femicides), targeted at a male audience and featuring men talking about domestic violence.  The Ministry of Women and Gender Equality, through the National Women's Service (SERNAM), operated women's centers, which provided legal and mental health support, and women's shelters.  The Ministry of Justice and PDI also operated several offices specifically dedicated to providing counseling and assistance in rape cases. SERNAM maintained partnerships with NGOs to provide training sessions for police officers and judicial and municipal authorities on the legal and psychological aspects of domestic violence.  The organization also continued to operate a 24-hour hotline for survivors of violence, including domestic abuse and rape.

Sexual Harassment:  Sexual harassment is not a criminal offense but is classified as a misdemeanor, with penalties outlined exclusively in the labor code.  By law sexual harassment is cause for immediate dismissal from employment.  The law requires employers to define internal procedures, or a company policy, for investigating sexual harassment, and employers may face fines and additional financial compensation to victims if it is shown that the company policy on sexual harassment was not followed.  The law provides protection to those affected by sexual harassment by employers and coworkers.  It also provides severance pay to individuals who resign due to sexual harassment if they have completed at least one year with the employer.

Reproductive Rights:  Couples and individuals have the right to decide the number, spacing, and timing of their children; manage their reproductive health; and have the information and means to do so, free from discrimination, coercion, and violence.  Access to sexual and reproductive health services and information was limited in remote regions, which especially affected poor women.  Emergency contraception is available at pharmacies without a prescription.

Discrimination:  Although women possess most of the same legal rights as men, discrimination in employment, pay, owning and managing businesses, and education persisted.  The default and most common marital arrangement is "conjugal society," which provides that a husband has the right to administer joint property, including his wife's property, without consultation or written permission from his spouse, but a wife must demonstrate that her husband has granted his permission before she is permitted to make financial arrangements.  Women married under the conjugal society arrangement were usually required to obtain permission from their husbands to apply for housing subsidies and take out loans or mortgages, while men had unrestricted access to these and other services.  Legislation remained pending years after a 2007 agreement with the IACHR to modify the conjugal society law to give women and men equal rights and responsibilities in marriage.  The commercial code provides that, unless a woman is married under the separate estate regime or a joint estate regime, she may not enter into a commercial partnership agreement without permission from her husband, while a man may enter into such an agreement without permission from his wife.  According to statistics from the civil registry, in 2012 (the most recent year available), 55 percent of couples married in Chile chose to enter into a conjugal society, 42.5 percent of couples chose a separate estate regime, and 2.5 percent chose a joint estate regime.

Despite a law providing for equal pay for equal work, the average woman's annual income was 32 percent less than that of men, according to the Ministry of Women and Gender Equality.  The ministry is in charge of protecting women's legal rights and is specifically tasked with combatting discrimination against women.  Women's centers throughout the country helped establish equal rights for women by offering services including training, counseling, and legal advice.

A June 3 ceremony launched the new cabinet-level Ministry of Women and Gender Equality.

**Children**

Birth Registration:  Citizenship is derived by birth within the country's territory and from one's parents or grandparents.  Births are registered immediately.

Child Abuse:  Intrafamily violence, including violence against children, remained a persistent problem.  Regional offices of the National Children's Service (SENAME) organized campaigns throughout the country to combat child abuse and the worst forms of child labor (also see section 7.c.).

The law renders persons convicted of child sexual abuse permanently ineligible for any position, job, career, or profession in educational settings requiring direct and habitual contact with children under age 18.  The law also includes a public registry of these sex offenders.

Early and Forced Marriage:  The legal minimum age of marriage is 18 (16 with parental consent).

Sexual Exploitation of Children:  Commercial sexual exploitation of children and adolescents was a problem, and children were exploited in prostitution with and without third-party involvement.  Law 20507 prohibits all forms of trafficking in persons, but internal child sexual exploitation cases were often prosecuted under a different law, Article 367 of the penal code, which provides lesser penalties.  Many convicted traffickers were released on parole or given suspended sentences, as permitted under sentencing guidelines for convictions with penalties of less than five years' imprisonment.  The range increases from five years and a day to 20 years and a fine of 31 to 35 UTM ($2,108 to $2,380) in cases where exploitation is habitual, or if there was deceit or abuse of authority or trust. (The monthly tax unit, or UTM, is a legally defined currency unit, indexed to inflation, equivalent to $68.)

Heterosexual sexual conduct with youths between ages 14 and 18 may be considered statutory rape depending on the circumstances; sex with a child under age 14 is considered rape, regardless of consent or the victim's gender. Penalties for statutory rape range from five to 20 years in prison. Child pornography is a crime. Penalties for producing child pornography range from 541 days to five years in prison.

Institutionalized Children: On September 13, the judicial branch published a report highlighting deficiencies, including overcrowding and chronic shortages of trained personnel, in institutions controlled by the country's child services organization, SENAME.

International Child Abductions: The country is a party to the 1980 Hague Convention on the Civil Aspects of International Child Abduction. See the Department of State's *Annual Report on International Parental Child Abduction* at travel.state.gov/content/childabduction/en/legal/compliance.html.

**Anti-Semitism**

The Jewish community numbered approximately 20,500. Jewish community leaders reported concern over the tone of social media postings which they perceived as threatening, although the commentary primarily referenced frustration with policies of the State of Israel and did not specifically mention either the Jewish people or Chilean Jews.

On August 18, the Palestinian Federation of Chile (FPDC) published on its Facebook site a cartoon depicting a figure smoking a missile cigar and sitting on a Star of David, the bottom point of which is sticking into the back of a dead Palestinian baby, as part of an article protesting the policies of the State of Israel. Following the September 28 death of former Israeli president Shimon Peres, the FPDC labeled him a "war criminal" on its official Twitter account.

**Trafficking in Persons**

See the Department of State's *Trafficking in Persons Report* at www.state.gov/j/tip/rls/tiprpt/.

**Persons with Disabilities**

The law prohibits discrimination against persons with physical, sensory, intellectual, and mental disabilities in employment, education, air travel and other transportation, access to health care, the judicial system, and the provision of other state services, and the government mostly enforced these provisions. Nevertheless, persons with disabilities suffered forms of de facto discrimination (also see section 7.d.). The law provides for universal and equal access to buildings, information, and communications. Most public buildings did not comply with legal accessibility mandates. The public transportation system, particularly outside Santiago, did not adequately provide accessibility for persons with disabilities. In recent years, however, TranSantiago, the main system of public transportation within Santiago, instituted changes to improve compliance with the law, including new ramp systems and elevators at certain metro stations as well as improved access to some buses. Nevertheless, many metro stations and most buses remained inaccessible to persons with physical disabilities.

The National Service for the Disabled (SENADIS) reported that children with disabilities attended school (primary and secondary) but noted difficulties in ensuring equal access to schooling at private institutions. SENADIS also reported that persons with disabilities had fewer opportunities to continue their education beyond secondary school.

SENADIS, which operates under the jurisdiction of the Ministry of Planning, has responsibility for protecting the rights of persons with disabilities, and advocates and promotes integration and protection policies throughout all government agencies.

**National/Racial/Ethnic Minorities**

Equal treatment and nondiscrimination are explicitly protected in the constitution, and the labor code specifically prohibits discrimination. According to the *Third National Survey of Human Rights*, published by the INDH in 2015, 61 percent of the surveyed population believed that people were discriminated against due to the color of their skin.

**Indigenous People**

Indigenous people have the right to participate in decisions affecting their lands, cultures, and traditions, including the exploitation of energy, minerals, timber, or other natural resources on indigenous lands.  The Citizen's Observatory reported, however, that indigenous people encountered serious obstacles to exercising these civil and political rights.  Indigenous people experienced societal discrimination, including in employment (also see section 7.d.), and there were reports of incidents in which they were attacked and harassed.  Indigenous women faced discrimination based on their gender, indigenous background, and reduced economic status, and they were especially vulnerable to violence, poverty, and illness.  Statistics as to whether or not indigenous people faced rates of violence different from the general population were not available.  The constitution does not specifically protect indigenous groups.

Protests by indigenous groups over land rights continued throughout the year, particularly in the Araucania region, one of the poorest regions and where one-third of the population self-identifies as belonging to the Mapuche indigenous group.  (Of the indigenous population, 80 percent belong to the Mapuche people.)  Protests over land rights sometimes included violent acts, such as the destruction of trucks and farm equipment and arson attacks on homes and farm structures.  Between January and June, the press reported that 18 rural churches in primarily Mapuche indigenous communities had been burned down by arsonists; some of the incidents were attributed to other Mapuche groups calling for land restitution.

There were numerous reports of police abuse against Mapuche individuals and communities, including against children.  The INDH brought petitions to protect the constitutional rights of Mapuche individuals, including children and adolescents, in cases of excessive use of force by security forces.  In addition the NGO Citizens' Observatory reported police searched Mapuche homes without warrants, arrested and released Mapuche individuals without detention control hearings (where individuals go before a judge to hear the charges against them to ensure their rights were protected and to decide if they should be held longer or released), and used intimidation and discriminatory statements against Mapuche individuals, including minors.

On March 13 the Supreme Court confirmed a Temuco Appellate Court ruling accepting an INDH petition to protect seven children, ages six months to nine years old, from the community of Rankilko who were subject to violence in November 2015 when they and their parents were forcibly removed by law enforcement from land that they had trespassed on and claimed as their own through squatter's rights, or adverse possession through occupation.  The ruling ordered the police to act within constitutional norms and respect the fundamental rights of the children; it also ordered them to open an internal investigation into the case.

In June the international NGO Center for Justice and International Law together with the local NGOs the Anide Foundation and the Mapuche Territorial Alliance published a report on the impact on children and adolescents of the repeated excessive use of force by security forces in two Mapuche communities in the Araucania region.  The report concluded that, despite protective actions and judicial rulings limiting police use of force, excessive use of force by security forces continued to affect children negatively.

The exploitation of energy, minerals, and timber occurred near indigenous communities, including mining projects in the north--where Aymara, Atacameno, Quechua, Colla, and Diaguita indigenous populations live--and timber exploitation in the south, where the Mapuche live.  Indigenous lands are demarcated, but some indigenous Mapuche communities demanded restitution of privately and publicly owned traditional lands.  Indigenous communities took legal action against mining projects in the north due to their potential contamination of the water supply and environment as well as the impact of demands for water in desert environments on subsistence agriculture.  Indigenous populations also expressed concern that timber plantations in the south could negatively affect the water table due to the introduction of nonnative species and the potential contamination of coastal areas from pulp production.

The Law on Indigenous Peoples' Protection and Development recognizes nine indigenous groups present in the country and creates an administrative structure to provide specialized programs and services to promote economic, social, and cultural development of these peoples.

**Acts of Violence, Discrimination, and Other Abuses Based on Sexual Orientation and Gender Identity**

The law sets the age of consent at 18 for homosexual sexual activity; heterosexual activity is permitted, under some circumstances, at age 14.  Antidiscrimination laws exist and prohibit discrimination based on sexual orientation or gender identity.  In February the NGO Movement for Homosexual Integration and Liberation (MOVILH) released its annual report, and noted that it tracked 258 cases of discrimination due to sexual orientation and gender identity during 2015.

Violence against LGBTI individuals continued.  According to MOVILH, in 2015 three persons were killed and 45 were physically assaulted in homophobic attacks.

Law enforcement authorities appeared reluctant to use the full recourse of a 2012 antidiscrimination law, including charging assailants of LGBTI victims with a hate crime, which would elevate criminal penalties as permitted under the law.

Laws prevent transgender persons from changing gender markers on government-issued identity documents, including national identity cards and university diplomas, to match their outward appearance or chosen expression.

**HIV and AIDS Social Stigma**

The law prohibits discrimination against persons based on their HIV status and provides that neither public nor private health institutions may deny access to health-care services on the basis of a person's serological status.  As the majority of citizens with HIV and AIDS are men, NGOs reported that government-sponsored outreach campaigns were oriented to a male audience, particularly men who have sex with men.  NGO reports noted that women faced obstacles to preventing HIV infection due to a lack of awareness surrounding transmission, understanding of access to public health services, and a limited ability to use protective measures such as condoms with their partners.  Some NGOs indicated that the rate of virus transmission may have increased among women and in indigenous communities, and they actively encouraged members of these groups to overcome social stigma and get tested.  During the year President Bachelet committed the government to ending mother-to-child transmission of HIV, in part by ensuring access to antiretroviral treatment for pregnant women.

**Section 7. Worker Rights**

**a. Freedom of Association and the Right to Collective Bargaining**

The law provides for the rights of workers, with some limitations, to form and join independent unions of their choice, bargain collectively, and conduct strikes.  The law also prohibits antiunion practices and requires either back pay or reinstatement for workers fired for union activity.

Police, military personnel, and civil servants working for the judiciary are prohibited from joining unions.  Union leaders are restricted from being candidates or members of congress.  The Directorate of Labor has broad powers to monitor unions' financial accounts and financial transactions. The law prohibits public employees from striking. While employees in the private sector have the right to strike, the law places some restrictions on this right. For example, an absolute majority of workers must approve strikes. Strikes by agricultural workers during the harvest season are prohibited. The law also prohibits employees of 101 private-sector companies, largely providers of services such as water and electricity, from striking, and it stipulates compulsory arbitration to resolve disputes in these companies. The law does not specifically prohibit employers from dismissing striking workers, but employers must show cause and pay severance benefits if they dismiss strikers. On August 29, the president signed into law revised labor standards to become effective in 2017. The legislation is designed to move Chile closer to international labor standards and includes a provision limiting the replacement of striking workers.

The law provides for collective bargaining rights only at the company level. Intercompany unions are permitted to bargain collectively only when the individual employers all agree to negotiate under such terms. The law does not provide for collective bargaining rights for workers in public institutions or in private institutions whose budget is dependent upon the Defense Ministry. It also does not provide for collective bargaining in companies whose employees are prohibited from striking, such as in health care, law enforcement, and public utilities. Whereas the previous labor code excluded collective bargaining rights for temporary workers or those employed solely for specific tasks, such as in agriculture, construction, ports, or the arts and entertainment sector, the recently revised labor standards eliminate these exclusions and therefore will allow collective bargaining by such workers starting in 2017.

The government generally enforced labor laws effectively. Nevertheless, the Labor Directorate under the Ministry of Labor commented on the need for more inspectors and noted that financial penalties did not always deter companies from repeating offenses. Companies are generally subject to sanctions for violations to the labor code of 1 to 10 UTM ($68 to $680) for micro- and small businesses, 2 to 40 UTM ($136 to $2,720) for medium businesses, and 3 to 60 UTM ($204 to $4,080) for large businesses, according to the severity of each case. Companies may receive "special sanctions" for infractions, which include antiunion practices. NGOs reported that cases in labor tribunals took on average three months to resolve. Cases involving fundamental rights of the worker often took closer to six months. NGOs continued to report that it was difficult for courts to sanction companies and order remedies in favor of workers for various reasons, including if a company's assets were in a different name or the juridical entity could not be located.

Freedom of association was generally respected. Employers sometimes did not respect the right to collective bargaining. Despite being prohibited by law, public-sector and health-care worker strikes occurred throughout the year. For example, the National Association of Public Workers called for a national strike on October 20 and 21 to demand the government increase its proposed wage adjustment for 2016. According to Freedom House and the International Trade Union Confederation, antiunion practices continued to occur. Employers continued to replace striking workers, which was permitted by law. NGOs and unions reported companies also used subcontracts and temporary contracts; they also obtained several fiscal registration/tax identification numbers as a form of antiunion discrimination and to increase the size of the workforce without granting collective bargaining rights.

The revised labor code, which will go into effect in 2017, provides that the labor court can require workers to resume work upon a determination that a strike, by its nature, timing, or duration, causes serious risk to health, national security, the supply of goods or services to the population, or to the national economy. Generally, a back-to-work order should apply only where a prolonged strike in a vital sector of the economy might cause a situation endangering the public's safety or health, and where applied to a specific category of workers.

**b. Prohibition of Forced or Compulsory Labor**

The law prohibits all forms of forced or compulsory labor. In general the government effectively enforced applicable laws. Penalties of five to 15 years' imprisonment for violations were sufficiently stringent to deter violations. NGOs reported many government officials responsible for identifying and assisting victims had limited resources and expertise to identify trafficking victims, particularly for forced labor. In addition, judges often suspended or commuted sentences. The government worked to prevent and combat forced labor through its anti-trafficking interagency taskforce of government agencies that includes international organizations and local NGOs. The task force developed and adopted a 2015-18 national action plan.

Forced labor continued to occur. Some foreign citizens were subjected to forced labor in the mining, agriculture, domestic service, and hospitality sectors. Some children were forcibly employed in the drug trade (see section 7.c.).

Also see the Department of State's *Trafficking in Persons Report* at
www.state.gov/j/tip/rls/tiprpt/.

### c. Prohibition of Child Labor and Minimum Age for Employment

The law sets the minimum age for employment at 18, although it provides that
children between 15 and 18 may work with the express permission of their parents
or guardians as long as they attend school.  They may perform only light work that
does not require hard physical labor or constitute a threat to health or the child's
development.  When attending school, children may not work more than 30 hours a
week and in no case more than eight hours a day or between the hours of 10 p.m.
and 7 a.m.  Employers must register their work contracts at the local Ministry of
Labor inspector's office.

Ministry of Labor inspectors effectively enforced regulations in the formal
economy but did not inspect or enforce such regulations in the informal economy.
Infractions included contracting a minor under 18 without the authorization of the
minor's legal representative, failure to register a minor's contract with the ministry,
and contracting a minor under age 15 for activities not permitted by law.  Penalties
and inspections were not generally seen as sufficient to deter grave violations that
mostly occurred clandestinely or in the informal economy.

The government devoted considerable resources and oversight to child labor
policies.  With accredited NGOs, SENAME ran programs throughout the country
to protect children in vulnerable situations.  SENAME, in coordination with labor
inspectors, identified and assisted children in abusive or dangerous situations.
SENAME continued to work with international institutions, such as the
International Labor Organization, and with other ministries to conduct training on
identifying and preventing the worst forms of child labor.  SENAME also
implemented public education programs to raise awareness and worked with the
International Labor Organization to operate rehabilitation programs for children
withdrawn from child labor.

Multisector government agencies continued to participate in the National Advisory
Committee to Eradicate Child Labor.  The committee met regularly throughout the
year and brought together civil society organizations and government agencies in a
coordinated effort to raise awareness, provide services to victims, and protect
victims' rights.  The Worst Forms of Child Labor Task Force, a separate entity,
maintained a registry of cases and developed a multisector protocol for the

identification, registration, and care of children and adolescents who are victims of commercial sexual exploitation. During the year SENAME worked with the National Tourism Service (SERNATUR) to include strict norms in hotel certification procedures for preventing the commercial sexual exploitation of children. This included special training for SERNATUR staff charged with assessing and certifying hotels.

Child labor continued to be a problem in the informal economy and agriculture, primarily in rural areas. Higher numbers of violations occurred in the construction, industrial manufacturing, hotels and restaurants, and agriculture sectors.

In urban areas it was common to find boys carrying loads in agricultural loading docks and assisting in construction activities, while girls sold goods on the streets and worked as domestic servants. Children worked in the production of ceramics and books and in the repair of shoes and garments. In rural areas, children were involved in caring for farm animals as well as harvesting, collecting, and selling crops, such as wheat. The use of children in illicit activities, which included the production and trafficking of narcotics, continued to be a problem. Commercial sexual exploitation of children also continued to be a problem (see section 6, Children).

Also see the Department of Labor's *Findings on the Worst Forms of Child Labor* at www.dol.gov/ilab/reports/child-labor/findings/.

### d. Discrimination with Respect to Employment and Occupation

The law and regulations prohibit employment discrimination based on race, sex, age, civil status, union affiliation, religion, political opinion, nationality, national extraction, social origin, disability, language, sexual orientation, and/or gender identity, HIV-positive status or other communicable diseases, or social status. The law also provides civil legal remedies to victims of employment discrimination based on race, ethnicity, nationality, socioeconomic situation, language, ideology or political opinion, religion or belief, association or participation in union organizations or lack thereof, gender, sexual orientation, gender identification, marriage status, age, affiliation, personal appearance, and sickness or physical disability.

The government effectively enforced applicable laws and regulations prohibiting employment discrimination. Authorities generally enforced the law in cases of sexual harassment, and there was no evidence of police or judicial reluctance to act.  Companies may receive "special sanctions" for infractions such as denying maternity leave.  Such penalties were generally sufficient to deter violations.

Nevertheless, discrimination in employment and occupation continued to occur.  Persons with disabilities often faced discrimination in hiring; they constituted approximately 7.6 percent of the working-age population but only 0.5 percent of the workforce.  Indigenous people experienced societal discrimination in employment.  Statistics regarding rates of discrimination faced by different groups were not available.

**e. Acceptable Conditions of Work**

The national minimum wage was 257,500 pesos ($380) a month for all occupations, including domestic servants.  The minimum monthly wage for workers over age 65 and under 18 was 192,230 pesos ($284).  The 2015 official extreme poverty level for one person was 91,274 pesos ($135) per month and the poverty level was 136,911 pesos per month ($202).

The law sets the legal workweek at six days or 45 hours.  The maximum workday is 10 hours (including two hours of overtime pay), but the law provides exemptions for hours of work restrictions for some categories of workers, such as managers; administrators; employees of fishing boats; restaurant, club, and hotel workers; drivers; airplane crews; telecommuters or employees who work outside of the office; and professional athletes.  The law mandates at least one 24-hour rest period during the workweek, except for workers at high altitudes, who may exchange a work-free day each week for several consecutive work-free days every two weeks.  Annual leave for full-time workers is 15 workdays, and workers with more than 10 years of service are eligible for an additional day of annual leave for every three years worked.  Overtime is considered to be any time worked beyond the 45-hour workweek, and workers are due time-and-a-half pay for any overtime performed.

The law establishes occupational safety and health standards, which are applicable to all sectors.  Special safety and health norms exist for specific sectors, such as mining and diving.  The National Service for Geology and Mines is further mandated to regulate and inspect the mining industry.  The law does not regulate the informal sector.  By law workers can remove themselves from situations that endanger health or safety without jeopardy to their employment, and authorities effectively protected employees in this situation.

The Labor Directorate under the Ministry of Labor is responsible for enforcing minimum wage and other labor laws and regulations, and it did so effectively in the formal economy. The Ministries of Health and Labor administered and effectively enforced occupational safety and health standards. The law establishes fines for noncompliance with labor regulations, including for employers who compel workers to work in excess of 10 hours a day or do not provide adequate rest days. Companies are generally subject to sanctions for violations to the labor code of 1 to 10 UTM ($68 to $680) for micro- and small businesses, 2 to 40 UTM ($136 to $2,720) for medium businesses, and 3 to 60 UTM ($204 to $4,080) for large businesses, according to the severity of each case. Companies may receive "special sanctions" for infractions such as causing irreversible injuries to an employee. Workers in the informal economy were not effectively protected in regard to wages or safety. Statistics regarding the number of workers involved in the informal economy were not available.

The Labor Directorate employed approximately 720 labor inspectors during the year. Both the Labor Directorate and NGOs reported the need for more inspectors to enforce labor laws throughout the country, particularly in remote areas. NGOs commented that inspectors and labor tribunal judges needed more training and that a lack of information and economic means generated an inequality between parties in cases before the tribunals. Fines were not considered to have a deterrent effect with larger employers. The Labor Directorate worked preventively with small and medium-sized businesses to assist in their compliance with labor laws.

Minimum wage violations were most common in the real estate and retail sectors. The sectors with the most infractions in safety and health standards were construction, retail, industrial manufacturing, and commerce. The service sector suffered the most accidents during the year. Immigrant workers in the agricultural sector were the group most likely to be subject to exploitative working conditions. On August 30, three mineworkers died in accidents at two different mines in northern Chile.